T0020485

GIANNIS ANTETOKOUNMPO

BY LUKE HANLON

Apex is distributed by North Star Editions:
sales@northstareditions.com | 888-417-0195

Produced for Apex by Red Line Editorial.

Photographs ©: Mark J. Terrill/AP Images, cover; Carlos Osorio/AP Images, 1, 18; Matt York/AP Images, 4–5; Ross D. Franklin/AP Images, 6, 8; Shutterstock Images, 9, 10–11, 14, 21; AP Images, 13; Kathy Willens/AP Images, 15; LM Otero/AP Images, 16–17; Kevin C. Cox/Pool Getty Images/AP Images, 20; Frank Franklin II/AP Images, 22–23; Paul Sancya/AP Images, 24–25, 29; Morry Gash/AP Images, 27

Library of Congress Control Number: 2022922223

ISBN
978-1-63738-552-4 (hardcover)
978-1-63738-606-4 (paperback)
978-1-63738-710-8 (ebook pdf)
978-1-63738-660-6 (hosted ebook)

Printed in the United States of America
Mankato, MN
082023

NOTE TO PARENTS AND EDUCATORS

Apex books are designed to build literacy skills in striving readers. Exciting, high-interest content attracts and holds readers' attention. The text is carefully leveled to allow students to achieve success quickly. Additional features, such as

TABLE OF CONTENTS

CHAPTER 1

ALLEY-OOP

t's Game 5 of the 2021 NBA Finals. The Milwaukee Bucks face the Phoenix Suns. The Bucks lead by one point. But the Suns have the ball with 20 seconds to go.

Game 5 of the 2021 NBA Finals took place on July 17.
Both teams had already won two games.

A Suns player drives into the lane. Milwaukee's Jrue Holiday steals the ball. He runs down the court and passes to Giannis Antetokounmpo.

FAST FACT

Giannis Antetokounmpo scored 32 points in Game 5 of the 2021 Finals.

Jrue Holiday often helped teammates score. He averaged 6.1 assists per game in 2020–21.

An alley-oop happens when a player catches the ball in the air and dunks it without touching the ground.

Antetokounmpo jumps and grabs the ball. He slams it through the hoop for a dunk. The Bucks win the game!

50-YEAR WAIT

In the NBA Finals, the first team to win four games is the **champion**. The Bucks did that in the sixth game of the **series**. It was their first championship since 1971.

The team that wins the NBA Finals receives the Larry O'Brien Trophy.

CHAPTER 2

EARLY LIFE

Giannis Antetokounmpo was born in Athens, Greece. He started playing basketball with his brothers when he was 13 years old.

Athens is the capital of Greece. It's also the

Giannis played on youth teams in Greece for three years. In 2011, he moved up to a **professional** team. NBA **scouts** started watching his games.

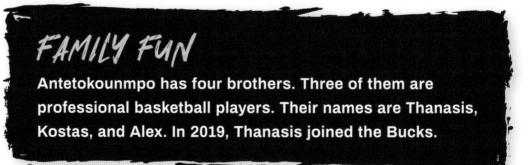

FAMILY FUN

Antetokounmpo has four brothers. Three of them are professional basketball players. Their names are Thanasis, Kostas, and Alex. In 2019, Thanasis joined the Bucks.

Giannis practices with his team in Athens during the 2012–13 season. ▶

Giannis was very tall, but some scouts thought he was too skinny for the NBA. The Milwaukee Bucks disagreed. They chose him in the 2013 NBA **Draft**.

The Bucks play at Fiserv Forum in Milwaukee, Wisconsin.

The Milwaukee Bucks picked Giannis in the first round of the 2013 NBA Draft.

FAST FACT

Some fans call Giannis the "Greek Freak." They say he has wildly good moves.

CHAPTER 3

ALL-STAR

Antetokounmpo grew even taller during his first year in the NBA. But he was still skinny. So, he worked to get stronger. That helped him play against bigger players.

By the end of his first NBA season, Antetokounmpo stood 6 feet, 11 inches (211 cm) tall.

Antetokounmpo got better every year. He led the Bucks to the **playoffs** several times. But they couldn't make it past the first round.

FAST FACT

Antetokounmpo became a great all-around player. He could block shots on defense and run fast to score on offense.

Antetokounmpo was named to his first NBA All-Star team during the 2016–17 season.

In both 2018–19 and 2019–20, the Bucks had the best **record** in the NBA. Still, they continued to struggle in the playoffs.

Antetokounmpo was voted the Defensive Player of the Year for the 2019–20 season.

Kareem Abdul-Jabbar was one of the best basketball players ever. He won the NBA MVP Award six times.

MVPs

Antetokounmpo won the NBA MVP Award in 2019 and 2020. He was only the second Bucks player ever to win it. Kareem Abdul-Jabbar was the first.

CHAPTER 4

NBA CHAMP

Antetokounmpo led the Bucks to the playoffs again in 2020–21. This time, they went all the way to the Finals.

The Bucks beat the Brooklyn Nets in the Eastern Conference Semifinals.

The Phoenix Suns won the first two games. But Antetokounmpo helped the Bucks win the next four. He also won Finals MVP.

GREAT GAME

Antetokounmpo had 50 points and 14 rebounds in Game 6 of the Finals. He became the seventh NBA player to score 50 points in a Finals game. He also blocked five shots.

Antetokounmpo celebrates after winning both the NBA Finals and the Finals MVP Award in 2021.

Antetokounmpo continued to dominate the next year. He became his team's top scorer of all time. Fans looked forward to what he would do next.

FAST FACT

As of 2023, Antetokounmpo had the most points, blocks, and **triple-doubles** in Bucks history.

Antetokounmpo's great play helped his team reach the playoffs again in 2022.

COMPREHENSION
QUESTIONS

Write your answers on a separate piece of paper.

1. Write a few sentences describing the main ideas of Chapter 2.

2. Antetokounmpo has won many awards. Which one do you think is the most impressive?

3. Which NBA team drafted Antetokounmpo?

    A. Milwaukee Bucks

    B. Phoenix Suns

    C. Los Angeles Lakers

4. Why could being skinny be a problem for an NBA player?

    A. Skinny players can't shoot as well.

    B. Skinny players can't run as fast.

    C. Skinny players can be easier to block or push.

5. What does **all-around** mean in this book?

*Antetokounmpo became a great **all-around** player. He could block shots on defense and run fast to score on offense.*

    A. good at all parts of the game
    B. only good at scoring
    C. bad at rebounding

6. What does **dominate** mean in this book?

*Antetokounmpo continued to **dominate** the next year. He became his team's top scorer of all time.*

    A. get hurt or sick
    B. be unable to score
    C. play very well

Answer key on page 32.

GLOSSARY

champion
A team that wins the final game in a conference or league.

draft
A system where professional teams choose new players.

playoffs
A set of games played after the regular season to decide which team will be the champion.

professional
Having to do with people who get paid for what they do.

record
The wins and losses that a team has during a season.

scouts
People who travel around to look for new, talented players.

series
A set of games played against the same team.

triple-doubles
Games when a player gets 10 or more in three categories, such as points, rebounds, and assists.

BOOKS

Flynn, Brendan. *Milwaukee Bucks All-Time Greats*. Mendota Heights, MN: Press Box Books, 2020.

Lilley, Matt. *The NBA Finals*. Mendota Heights, MN: Apex Editions, 2023.

Lowe, Alexander. *G.O.A.T. Basketball Power Forwards*. Minneapolis: Lerner Publications, 2023.

ONLINE RESOURCES

Visit **www.apexeditions.com** to find links and resources related to this title.

ABOUT THE AUTHOR

Luke Hanlon is a sportswriter and editor based in Minneapolis. He grew up in Illinois and regularly watches Giannis torture his hometown Chicago Bulls.

INDEX

ANSWER KEY:
1. Answers will vary; 2. Answers will vary; 3. A; 4. C; 5. A; 6. C